Life in a French Town

Life in a
FRENCH TOWN

written and illustrated by

D. L. ELLIS

GEORGE G. HARRAP & CO. LTD
London   Toronto   Wellington   Sydney

First published in Great Britain 1968
by GEORGE G. HARRAP & CO. LTD
182 High Holborn, London, W.C.1

Reprinted 1969

Composed in Monophoto Ehrhardt and printed by
William Clowes and Sons, Limited, London and Beccles
Made in Great Britain

Preface

Sereinbourg is an imaginary French town in an imaginary part of France. As far as possible, however, Sereinbourg represents a typical community, and the information contained in this book is factual and authentic. The illustrations are based mainly on photographs of existing buildings in provincial France.

The book is primarily designed to serve pupils in the second and third years of Secondary Modern Schools and the middle grades of Comprehensive Schools.

These are children to whom the learning of French does not come easily. They require a great deal of encouragement, especially in the second and third years, when the novelty of learning a foreign language begins to diminish.

One source of encouragement comes from interest lessons. There is every justification for a special weekly or fortnightly interest lesson, since learning about France is just as important as learning French; but most French textbooks do not seriously take this into account.

Many teachers do not have sufficient material ready to hand to justify a whole lesson being devoted to interest work, with the result that interest lessons cease to exist soon after their initiation.

Sereinbourg would provide plenty of material, sufficient to encourage a teacher to allot a definite lesson each week, or every fortnight, to interest work. Not only would Sereinbourg provide a ready-made theme of work for the year, but it could also be a possible source of inspiration for project work on points arising from each section.

As far as possible each section is planned to cover one, two, or three lessons. Firstly, the text of the chosen section is read aloud by individual pupils. The teacher can then add facts which he has acquired through his own experience and which he believes relevant to the subject. Each teacher is more than likely to have knowledge which he cannot easily convey to children in grammar and conversation lessons, but Sereinbourg would enable him to use his own information. Finally, we have the active part of the lesson for the children. The list of suggestions at the back of the book provides for this.

Although each section may be regarded as complete in itself, additional material and information can be used. The list of suggestions for teachers contains ideas which might not occur to them.

The text of the book is in English. A French text would have to be very simple to enable children to understand it, and much of the interest would have to be eliminated because it could not be expressed in simple French. However, the essential French vocabulary which has been included might prove useful in oral work connected with town life.

The material for this book was collected during a two-year stay in France and on subsequent visits. It has been used in the classroom with second- and third-year children, and the activities have proved successful.

Thanks are due to my wife, whose help has been invaluable in the writing of this book.

D. L. E.

Contents

[8]

Introduction

Le Plan de la Ville

Sereinbourg was first established as an agricultural community during the early Middle Ages, at a bend in the river **Serein**. The river provided a natural defence on two sides and a natural means of transport. It also supplied water for farming as well as drinking. Wooden defences were constructed from the areas now known as **Place Clemenceau** and **Place du Marché** to the crest of the knoll which is now **Place de la Nation**. The oldest part of the present town, **le vieux quartier**, is therefore within those limits described. Le vieux quartier of Sereinbourg has escaped destruction and demolition to some extent through the ages, so that the streets still tend to be narrow and winding.

As the population increased and the community became more important, the settlement took its present name and expanded away from the river. New boundary walls were built along the line of the **Boulevard Gambetta**, as it now is. The Sereinbourg market became the centre of much trading in the region at this time, and the stone church was erected. A **bourg** was considered to be the principal village in the district, and had in it the Town Hall and church, which served the smaller outlying villages. By the middle of the nineteenth century, Sereinbourg, which already had the status of a town, had expanded to its present limits, indicated by the exterior boulevard.

There is nearly always an obvious sense of planning about French towns. Arterial roads pass directly through the town, while one or more complete ring roads help to prevent congestion by facilitating the movement of traffic round it. This idea of certain roads passing directly through and other roads circling the town originated in Paris during the nineteenth century, and was copied throughout France. The system is also used abroad, especially in the modern cities of America. Furthermore, French towns make the best artistic use of their rivers by constructing picturesque quaysides, with roads running along the edge of the water. The method of

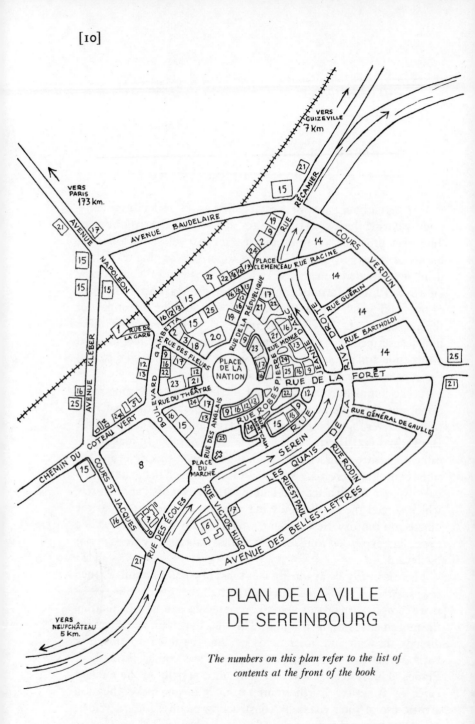

PLAN DE LA VILLE
DE SEREINBOURG

*The numbers on this plan refer to the list of
contents at the front of the book*

naming streets does not alter very much from town to town. The **boulevards, rues, chemins, cours,** and **places** are usually named after local and national heroes, politicians, generals, artists, poets, sculptors, novelists, saints, and historical events.

La Gare

French railways are known by the initials **S.N.C.F.**, which stand for **Société Nationale des Chemins de fer Français**. The railways were developed more slowly in France than in England. Hence French planners, engineers, and technicians were able to benefit from the mistakes of English pioneers. The most obvious benefit can be seen in the simplicity of the French system of main lines, known as **les grandes relations**.

Nevertheless, many differences exist because of different customs and attitude towards life.

Let us first look at a plan of a French railway station, showing its main features. The key for the plan is set out below:

a. **les voies ferrées**
b. **les quais**
c. **le porteur**
d. **le passage souterrain**
e. **les colis**
f. **la salle d'attente**
g. **le buffet**
h. **la consigne**
i. **les guichets et renseignements**
j. **l'entrée**
k. **la sortie**
l. **tabac**
m. **le bureau du chef de gare**
n. **le parking**
o. **la cour**
p. **les taxis**
q. **la rue**

The station platforms are very low. In order to board the train passengers have to climb the steps built into the carriage door. At many of the smaller stations travellers are not permitted on the platform until a few minutes before the arrival of the train. As the train comes into sight there is usually a warning voice on the loudspeaker: **"Attention, attention, le train entre en gare."**

Tickets for travel are either **billet simple** or **billet aller-retour**.

There are several classifications for trains. **Un autorail** (or **train automoteur**) is a light diesel train. **Un omnibus** is a stopping train. **Un express** is fast, stopping at the main stations. **Un rapide** is a real express train which stops only at the very important stations. **Un train direct** is a non-stop, through train.

PLAN DE LA GARE

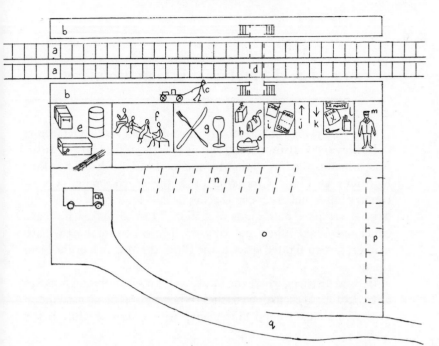

In a French train passengers soon become acquainted with certain warning notices such as: **Défense de fumer** or **Non-fumeurs**, **Défense de se pencher au dehors**, and **Eau non potable**.

Many people travelling overnight like to sleep in relative comfort, and so they hire a **couchette**. Certain compartments can be converted into six couchettes—three simple bunks on each side, one above the other. Passengers may sleep fully clothed.

All the information necessary for rail travel is contained in a book which can be bought at the station. If you wish to buy one for your region, you ask for **un Chaix**. There are five railway regions in France: Ouest, Nord, Est, Sud-Est Méditerranée, and Sud-Ouest, with Paris as the common point of contact for each one. Chaix gives information and times for trains not only in your particular region but also for trains on all main lines throughout France, and for trains on link-up routes with other countries like Spain, Italy, Germany, Belgium, and Switzerland. Chaix also helps you calculate the length of your journey in **kilomètres** so that you can estimate the cost before buying the ticket at the **guichet**.

Numéro 2

La Gare d'Autobus et la Gare Routière

On the plan of Sereinbourg the number 2 at the intersection of **Boulevard Gambetta** and **rue des Fleurs** is the **Gare d'Autobus,** which is the bus station for the local bus service. The **Gare Routière** at **Place Clemenceau** is the coach station. Cross-country buses and excursion coaches usually leave from here. Only large towns have both kinds of station. Most towns usually have either one or the other, and very small towns in rural areas have neither; just an allotted space in the **Place du Marché,** or the main square.

In rural districts, where the bus service may be infrequent, buses often do duty as excursion coaches. When a bus is being used for an excursion a small round blue plaque with a vertical white bar is

L'AUTOBUS

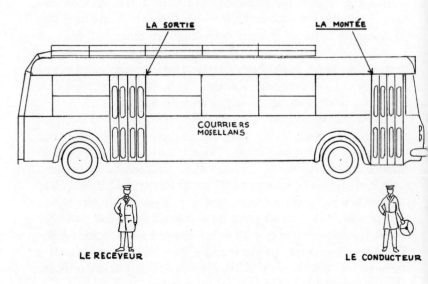

LA SORTIE   LA MONTÉE

COURRIERS MOSELLANS

LE RECEVEUR   LE CONDUCTEUR

fixed on the back. When the bus returns to its ordinary service the blue plaque is reversed and the red side shows.

The name for a bus is **autobus,** and the name for a coach is **auto-car,** but people often refer to both simply as **le car.**

French buses have only one deck, and there is usually more space for standing than for sitting. This enables a great many passengers to get into a fairly small area during the 'rush hour' (**heure d'affluence**). At such times travelling can be very uncomfortable, and it can also be very difficult for a passenger to reach the exit in time to alight at the bus-stop (**l'arrêt**).

Smoking is usually forbidden, although a standing space may sometimes be reserved at the back of the bus for smokers.

In many buses a conductor is a luxury, and very often there is just the driver, who has to collect the fares as passengers board the vehicle. French people are not accustomed to forming queues at bus-stops; they usually stand in groups. However, everyone manages to squeeze on because there seems to be no limit to the number of people a bus will carry. Passengers are always considerate to invalids and disabled and old people, and there are seats specially reserved for them in buses.

Le Syndicat d'Initiative

This small building in the **rue des Fleurs** is the Information Office. This one has been specially built for its purpose, although in other towns the **Syndicat d'Initiative** may be situated in part of

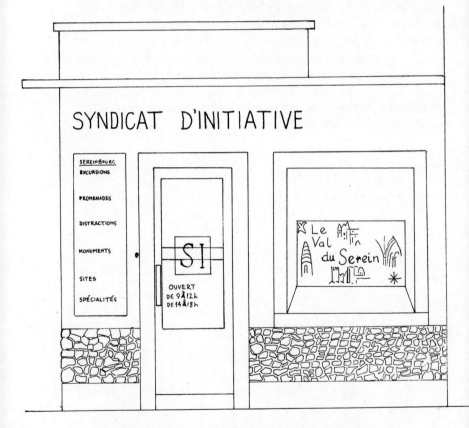

LE SYNDICAT D'INITIATIVE, RUE DES FLEURS.

another building. In any case it is always located near the centre of a town, so that visitors can easily find it. Most visitors call here first in order to obtain information about the town. There is absolutely no reason why a visitor to a French town should remain a stranger for more than ten minutes after arrival at the local Syndicat d'Initiative.

The first thing to ask for is a plan of the town. This will show all the public buildings, such as the Town Hall, the Post Office, and the Chamber of Commerce. Churches and monuments are shown, and pleasant walks in and around the town may also be marked. However, the visitor has other needs besides taking in all the sights. He has to eat and sleep, and therefore would want to obtain a list of hotels and restaurants. The Syndicat can provide these lists, and to save the visitor another journey to the Information Office the assistant will probably give him some leaflets about the local bus services, sporting facilities, and evening entertainments.

French people are extremely proud of their countryside, which is very varied and beautiful, and it is not difficult for a stranger to appreciate this since there are many excursions and tours organized. The Syndicat can supply all the necessary details concerning these trips, and even provide maps of the region showing all the historical buildings and places of interest.

Before leaving Sereinbourg the tourist can pay a final visit to the Syndicat d'Initiative to gather some information about the next town he is going to visit.

Numéros 4, 5, 6, et 7

Les Écoles

4

L'ÉCOLE MATERNELLE

The **École Maternelle** accepts children between the ages of two and six, but schooling at this age is not compulsory. The children learn through playing games, and this helps them when they start at their first real school.

5

L'ÉCOLE PRIMAIRE

French children have to start school at the age of six, and they stay at the **École Primaire** until they are eleven years old. The boys and girls now learn to read, write, do arithmetic, paint, and sing. It is very much like being at a junior school in England.

6

LE COLLÈGE D'ENSEIGNEMENT GÉNÉRAL

At the age of eleven children go to their senior school, where they have to remain until they are sixteen. Boys and girls who would benefit from the short five-year course go to the **Collège d'Enseignement Général**; then at the age of sixteen they can go out to work.

7

LE LYCÉE

Many children go to the **Lycée** at the age of eleven. These are the ones who would benefit from a longer course of study, and they stay at school after the age of sixteen to try to gain a place at university or training college or some other establishment for higher education.

At the Lycée the Principal, **le Proviseur** or **le Directeur**, is in charge of administrative matters. There are also two other Principals. **Le Censeur** is responsible for organizing the timetable and the academic life of the school. **L'Intendant** looks after the financial aspect of the school. These three Principals do not teach; they have sufficient work to occupy them in their offices, and each requires at least one secretary. With regard to discipline, the **Surveillant-Général** is responsible for administering punishments and preventing bad behaviour. He has a number of assistants, known as **Surveillants**, who have to be on duty in all parts of the school. Surveillants, or **Pions**, are usually young men and women who wish to earn money at the school while studying at the local university.

Many Lycées have boarders, and it is therefore necessary for some of the Pions to live at the school in the **Internat**, which is the name for the boarding house.

Very often the Proviseur, Censeur, Intendant, Surveillant-Général, and even the secretaries live at the Lycée as well. They have their own house or **appartement** in the school grounds.

The **Concierge** (caretaker) also has accommodation in the school. At night, when the Concierge has finished his work, the **Veilleur de nuit** comes on duty. The Veilleur de nuit has the

LES ÉCOLES

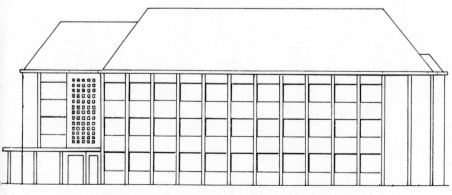

A TEACHING BLOCK AT A TYPICAL MODERN LYCÉE

lonely task of patrolling the buildings and the grounds to ensure that everything is safe.

In France schoolchildren commence their secondary studies in **la classe de sixième**, and progress through the years until they reach **la classe de seconde**, and finally **la classe de première**. Children who do not pass the annual examinations have to stay in the same form for another year. This encourages them to work hard, as no-one likes to spend two years in one class.

During their first two years at the Lycée the children are watched carefully by the teachers, whose task it is to make a progress report on them. Having considered the progress report, parents then have to decide which course of study would be most suitable for their children. They can choose one of the three sections into which the Lycée is divided. In the **section classique** the emphasis is on Greek, Latin, and two modern languages. In the **section moderne** pupils concentrate more on their own language and two modern languages. In the **section technique** more time is devoted to the sciences.

In the **classe de première** pupils take the first **baccalauréat**, and in the **classe de philosophie** or **mathématiques** they take the second **baccalauréat**, which is similar to the G.C.E., Advanced Level. As you can see on the school timetable, French schoolchildren seem to work much harder than English schoolchildren.

EXAMPLE OF A SCHOOL TIMETABLE FOR ONE DAY

ENGLISH SCHOOL		FRENCH SCHOOL	
Time	*Timetable*	*L'heure*	*Emploi du temps*
9.00–9.15	Assembly	8.00	Musique
9.15–9.20	Registration	9.00	
9.20–10.00	Music	9.00	Histoire
10.00–10.40	History	10.00	
10.40–10.50	Break	10.00–10.05	Récréation
10.50–11.30	French	10.05	Français
11.30–12.05	Geography	11.05	
12.05–1.15	Lunch-time	11.05 12.05	Géographie
1.15–1.20	Registration	12.05–2.00	Déjeuner
1.20–2.00 2.00–2.35	Art	2.00 3.00	Dessin
2.35–2.45	Break	3.00	Anglais
2.45–3.25	English	4.00	
3.25–4.00	Maths	4.00 5.00	Mathématiques

Numéro 8

Le Parc

Sereinbourg is fortunate in having a particularly fine park. All French towns have a park, but not necessarily with a lake or botanical garden or zoological garden.

In the nineteenth century Emperor Napoléon III decided that Paris should have the finest parks and gardens in Europe. He found the best designers and gardeners in France to make his dream come true. There was much activity: plans were drawn up, lakes were excavated, trees were transplanted from the countryside, paths were laid, soil was moved and landscaped, and public amenities were installed. As a result, Paris now has the Bois de Boulogne, the Parc Monceau, the Parc de Montsouris, the Parc des Buttes-Chaumont, and the Bois de Vincennes. Napoléon III's idea was to bring the countryside into his capital city to make it beautiful, and also to provide green open spaces for the Parisians to walk and play in. He believed that this would make them much happier people.

In the course of time other French cities followed this example. The big cities could afford to create large and interesting parks, whereas the small towns had to be content with more modest results. However, the people were very pleased to have somewhere to relax on Sundays and summer evenings, without having to take a train or bus ride to the country.

In the **Parc Napoléon Premier** it is specially interesting that the town secured the services of Bartholdi to carve the statue of Napoléon Bonaparte. Notice also the display of trees. When the park was created in 1869 the specialists chose two kinds of poplar to border the two sides by the **Cours St-Jacques** and the **Chemin du Coteau Vert**. Certain species of pine and oak were selected for the wood. The ruined tower in the centre of the wood is a legacy from the Middle Ages.

LE PARC NAPOLÉON PREMIER

CHEMIN DU COTEAU VERT

COURS ST JACQUES

BOULEVARD GAMBETTA

LYCÉE

TERRAIN
DE
SPORTS

a.	les allées	h.	les îles
b.	le bois	i.	le pédalo
c.	les sentiers	j.	le chalet (café-restaurant)
d.	la tour (ruine—12e siècle)	k.	la statue de Napoléon 1er
e.	le jardin botanique	l.	les pelouses
f.	les serres	m.	le jardin zoologique
g.	le lac	n.	le jardin des enfants

Les Boules

Since the paths in the park are made of gravel, bowls players go there whenever possible to have a game of **Boules**. A similar game is **la Pétanque**, played chiefly in the South of France. French bowls are made of metal, and they are thrown, not rolled. The game takes place on a gravel surface, never on a beautifully flat lawn as in England. The bowls, weighing about 2 lb each, are thrown with a great deal of back-spin, so that they will bite into the gravel and remain where they land. This is extremely difficult to do successfully, and passers-by often crowd round to consider the skill of the players and the state of the game.

Two players or two teams compete in the game. The first player throws the little wooden ball (**cochonnet**) a few yards in front of him, scores a line in the gravel with his heel, and throws his first bowl to arrive as close as possible to the cochonnet. His opponent stands behind the line and throws his first bowl, aiming to get even closer to the cochonnet. The player farther from the cochonnet has his second turn. The other player then throws his second bowl, and finally both men examine the result. The player whose bowl is closest to the cochonnet gains one point. If both of his bowls are nearer the cochonnet than either bowl of his opponent, then he scores two points.

It is permissible for bowls to strike each other on the ground. Indeed, part of the skill in the game is to knock the opponent's bowls out of the way of the cochonnet. The winner of the first game begins the next game, and play goes on like this until the first man reaches fifteen points. The overall winner is decided after three sets.

Numéro 9

Le Café

Cafés are a very important part of any French town because people regard them as places to meet their friends or to relax. The friendly atmosphere encourages people to linger until late in the evening. Alcoholic drinks, such as beer and wine, are served at any time, as well as the usual drinks and snacks. In France cafés remain open all day, and many of them do not close until the last customer has decided to go home. Some cafés provide a juke-box, pin-tables, table-top football, or television.

Customers do not normally go to the bar to be served. They choose their table and call the waiter (**le garçon**). The white-coated waiters are very efficient and skilful, because they take a great pride in their work. It is most unusual to see a waitress (**une serveuse**), as serving in a café is generally regarded as a man's job. When the drinks are served the bill (**l'addition**) is also put on the table. Customers are expected to leave a tip, which should be between 10 per cent and 15 per cent of the bill. If the service charge (**le service**) is included SERVICE COMPRIS will be printed on the bill.

The price of drinks usually varies according to where the customer has his refreshment. It is slightly cheaper to have a cup of coffee at the bar than at a table on the terrace.

La terrasse is an important feature of the café, because in the warm months people like to sit outside with their drinks and watch the passers-by. On each side of the terrace there are usually **jardinières**, which are boxes filled with earth and planted with flowers or shrubs. **La banne**, the awning, can be pulled out to provide shade. During the winter the larger cafés maintain their terrace on the pavement by enclosing it with glass partitions so that customers can still sit 'outside'. **Un poêle**, a stove, is installed to make the terrace warm and cosy.

In the picture you can also see a cigar-shaped symbol displayed above the awning. The symbol is always red and signifies that tobacco, cigarettes, and postage-stamps are on sale inside. A café

[25]

LE CAFÉ RUE DE LA RÉPUBLIQUE—PLACE DE LA NATION
SPRING AND SUMMER

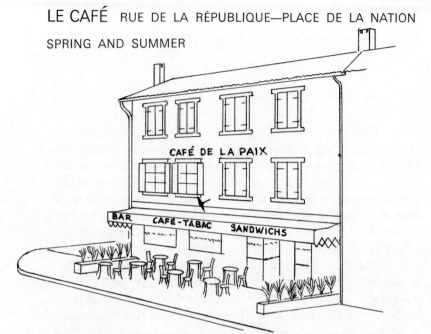

LE CAFÉ RUE DE LA RÉPUBLIQUE—PLACE DE LA NATION
AUTUMN AND WINTER

which provides this service is usually known as a **café-tabac**. Another name for a café is **un bistro**. **Une brasserie**, however, provides hot meals as well as drinks.

Tea is not a favourite drink. It is classed as **une infusion**. An infusion is made by soaking a tea-bag in a glass of hot water. The water extracts the goodness from the leaves in the bag, and the liquid is sweetened before being drunk. (**Une tisane** is another name for this kind of drink, but also indicates that it is medicinal.) **Un thé**, therefore, is served like this and is very weak. **Un thé au lait** is served with a small jug of hot or cold milk, and a **thé au citron** has a slice of lemon in it. Cafés which are used to English visitors usually understand how to make tea as we know it, in a teapot with a jug of cold milk. Other infusions are **verveine** (vervain), **tilleul** (lime-blossom tea), **menthe** (mint tea), **oranger** (orange-blossom tea), and **camomille** (camomile tea).

Cocoa, however, is made in the same way as in England, although it is called **chocolat**, and is usually drunk at breakfast-time.

When a Frenchman orders coffee he expects to get black coffee made from coffee beans. **Un café** is the word for coffee, but customers sometimes ask for **café noir, café nature, café express,** or **café filtre**, although all these names have the same meaning. **Un café filtre** is slightly different in that an empty cup with a metal container on it is brought to the table. The metal container has ground coffee and hot water in it. The water soaks through the ground coffee and drops through the filter into the cup. Coffee cups are very small, and cubes of sugar are put on the saucer. Sugar is wrapped, and the name of the sugar refinery is printed on the wrapper. The more fashionable cafés even have their name printed on the paper.

White coffee is called **café-crème**, but only a small amount of hot milk or cream is added. **Un grand café-crème** is served in a large cup. Most cafés serve breakfast coffee, which is known as **café au lait**—half coffee, half milk. Instant coffee may be used for this, and it is served in a special bowl or a large cup. **Un café complet** is the order to make for breakfast. This would include **café au lait** and **croissants**, which are crescent-shaped rolls, or **tartines**, which are long slices of bread. Butter and jam may be provided as well.

Pure fruit juices are called **jus de fruits,** and the most usual ones are **orange, pamplemousse** (grapefruit), **ananas** (pineapple), and **raisins** (grapes). **Boissons gazeuses** are fizzy drinks, such as orange, citron, or limonade (lemonade). Un diablo menthe is a mixture of mint cordial and lemonade, which is especially refreshing on hot days. Citron pressé is fresh lemon juice with water and sugar added, and orange pressée is fresh orange juice diluted in the same way.

Beer comes mainly from the north-east of France and from Germany. The usual order is un demi, which is about half a pint of pale beer, either à la pression (draught) or en bouteille (bottled). Bière brune is brown beer, and customers have to be precise if they want this sort.

Wine is far more popular and less expensive than beer. Since France is the main wine-growing country in the world, the best wines are available in French cafés. The choice is between vin rouge (red wine), vin rosé (pink wine), vin blanc sec (dry white wine), and vin blanc doux (sweet white wine). Un kir makes a change from wine by itself; it is a mixture of cassis (blackcurrant) and vin blanc doux.

France is also famous for its spa towns, which produce eau minérale, mineral water. Mineral waters are sometimes named after the town they come from, and a good selection is on sale in most cafés.

Apéritifs and liqueurs are strong alcoholic drinks, of which there are many varieties. Apéritifs are drunk before meals to stimulate the appetite, and liqueurs are taken after meals to help the digestion.

Winter drinks include un vin chaud and un grog. Un vin chaud is made from vin rouge and hot water with a slice of lemon, and sugar. Un grog is similar, except that rum is used instead of red wine.

Sandwiches are the usual form of snack. There are sandwich au jambon (ham), sandwich au fromage (cheese), and sandwich au saucisson sec (dry sausage). French sandwiches are long and crusty, quite different from sandwiches in England. CASSE-CROÛTE À TOUTE HEURE may be written up outside a café which offers more ambitious snacks at any time of day.

La Rue

LA RUE
BOULEVARD GAMBETTA SEEN FROM PLACE CLEMENCEAU

The picture shows a deserted street very early in the morning, when most of the shutters are still closed. The character of a French street depends to a large extent on the everyday bustle of

people and vehicles, but even without them there are many characteristics which make it different from an English street.

A few streets may still have a cobbled surface. French cobble-
stones are smooth and arranged in patterns, and the ride over them
is not too rough.

Le passage clouté is the pedestrian crossing marked out with
metal studs. There are neither black-and-white stripes nor beacons,
although yellow stripes are sometimes painted. It is not necessarily
safe to cross the road at this point, but if a pedestrian were knocked
down on such a crossing he would be considered free from
blame.

Traffic lights (**les feux de circulation**) are similar to ours, but
they may be left flashing at amber after the rush-hour at the less
dangerous places. There are some traffic lights which consist of only
one flashing amber light. These are installed in some back streets
where a warning of possible danger is necessary.

Many of the drains are narrow openings in the kerb. These are
accompanied by an inspection cover on the pavement. It is often
possible to see very small round manholes on the pavement. These
are used on special occasions, when the cover is removed so that
flagpoles can be inserted in the hole. At Christmas-time real or
imitation fir-trees can be put in the holes to decorate the street.
Other decorations such as bunting and coloured lights may be
strung across the road.

In England we expect pavements to be even because we are
accustomed to standard paving-stones. In France the pavements
are more interesting. They may be made of asphalt or paving-stones
of varying size and colour, usually laid in different patterns. Many
pavements away from the main roads may simply be made of
cinders or gravel, with kerbing-stones to keep them tidy.

Rubbish-bins are nearly always put on the edge of the pavement
on the day when the dustmen make their round. The standard bin
(**la poubelle**) is rather small, and it is quite normal to see the whole
length of the kerb lined with them.

Trees are an accepted sight in all towns. They help to bring the
feeling of the countryside into urban areas. Plane-trees (**le platane**)
are regarded as the best kind of tree because they provide plenty of
shade and their leaves are easily cleaned by rain, thereby preserving
their freshness. Also, the bark of this tree peels by itself periodically,
taking the soot and grime with it. In some towns a circular metal
grille covers the earth surrounding the tree, allowing rain to get to

the roots and also keeping the pavement even. Other trees such as the lime (**le tilleul**) are equally popular in towns.

The post supporting the electric cables (**le poteau électrique**) in the foreground of the picture is a design which is frequently seen in France, but it is by no means the only sort. As far as possible, the French use wall brackets, attached high on buildings, to carry electricity wires. This does away with unsightly posts and makes the wires more inconspicuous. Street lights (**le réverbère**) are often fixed to buildings or on existing posts and brackets. This is another way of keeping the pavement clear.

Outside the town most roads are constructed and repaired by the **Département** (something like an English county). These are known as 'D' roads, but they are not the best type of French road. **Une Route Nationale** is a main road and marked as an 'N' road on maps and signposts. **Routes Nationales** are built and maintained by the Government, as are **Autoroutes**, which are similar to British motorways.

French road signs are divided into three groups.

The first group consists of warning signs, which are triangular.

They have red edges, a yellow background, and blue symbols in the middle.

Here are eight of the most usual warning signs :

 This sign is an exception to the rule because the edges may be either red or blue, although the meaning is the same. Drivers must stop at the major road ahead. Sometimes there is a plaque above this sign which says: **STOP À 150 m**

 Intersection. This sign means that drivers must give way to the traffic coming from the right. At very dangerous crossroads drivers are reminded of this by the words **PRIORITÉ À DROITE** written on a plaque under the sign.

 Intersection. Drivers who pass this sign have the right of way at the crossroads.

 Danger. The warning underneath this sign varies according to the danger. In a mountainous region where there is danger from falling rocks a warning: **CHUTES DE PIERRES** may be attached under the sign. In areas of France where there are likely to be icy patches the sign will have **RISQUE DE VERGLAS** written underneath it.

 Chaussée Glissante. This sign is used as a warning where the road surface is usually slippery.

 Virage à Droite. Right-hand bend. The arrow is obviously turned the other way for a left-hand bend.

Virages. A double bend is indicated here. If the road has many bends over a long distance the words **VIRAGES SUR 1,7 Km** may be added.

Chaussée Rétrécie. Road narrows.

The second group forbids drivers to do certain things.

These signs are circular and have a thick red rim.

Five of the most frequently seen prohibition signs are shown below :

Sens Interdit. The No Entry sign has a white horizontal bar.

Stationnement Interdit. The No Parking sign has a red bar on a blue background.

Virage à Gauche Interdit. No Left Turn has a white background and a blue arrow on a red bar.

Signaux Sonores Interdits. This sign forbids the sounding of motor-horns. The horn on the sign is blue and the background white.

On the Halt sign the word STOP is blue, the triangle red, and the background white.

[34]

The third kind of sign is also circular, but it is blue and white, showing drivers what they must do.

The following two signs give compulsory directions to drivers :

Sens Obligatoire. The One-Way sign has a white arrow.

Sens Giratoire. This roundabout sign also has white arrows.

Poteau Indicateur.

Signposts are white with blue lettering and blue edging.

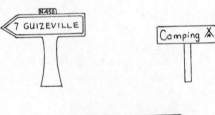

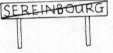

The sign showing the name of the town is displayed for motorists as they drive into a town. As they drive out of it they see a similar sign with the name crossed out. Strangers find this sort of sign particularly useful.

La Boulangerie

La Boulangerie is the shop where bread is both made and sold. Since French bread tends to go stale rather quickly, it has to be bought and eaten on the same day. Most bakers make bread twice a day in the bakery which is usually behind the shop. In this way there is always a ready supply of fresh bread. The picture shows the most popular items of bread that the baker sells, but there are other variations, and the names may be different according to the region. The drawings overleaf are not to scale.

Un croissant, which is a breakfast roll, takes its name from its shape, and is a mixture of puff pastry and bread. It begins as a flat triangle of pastry which is gently rolled up from the base. The ends are then curved round to make a crescent shape. French housewives can either go out to buy these croissants early in the morning before breakfast or buy them on the previous evening. If croissants are bought in the evening they need to be warmed in the oven for ten minutes before breakfast to make them fresh again. They are best eaten with butter and apricot preserves. **Un croissant fourré**, similar in shape, and having a filling of almond paste, is also a breakfast roll. **Une brioche** is a different sort of roll which originated in Normandy. **Un petit pain au chocolat** is made of puff pastry which is rolled up round a finger of chocolate, and is usually eaten at breakfast as an alternative to croissants. **Un petit pain** is an ordinary bread roll.

Any of these rolls may also be eaten after school when the children come home hungry. The French do not have tea-time as we know it, but there is a meal known as **le goûter** which the children have at about five o'clock. It consists of **café au lait**, **café-crème**, or **chocolat**, with a roll or a slice of bread.

The crust of a loaf is a good indication of its freshness. It ought to be **croustillant**, which means crisp, and it should crackle when pressed between the fingers, whereas the crust of a stale loaf is soft. Shoppers usually have to carry bread in their hands, as the loaves

LA BOULANGERIE
RUE JEANNE D'ARC

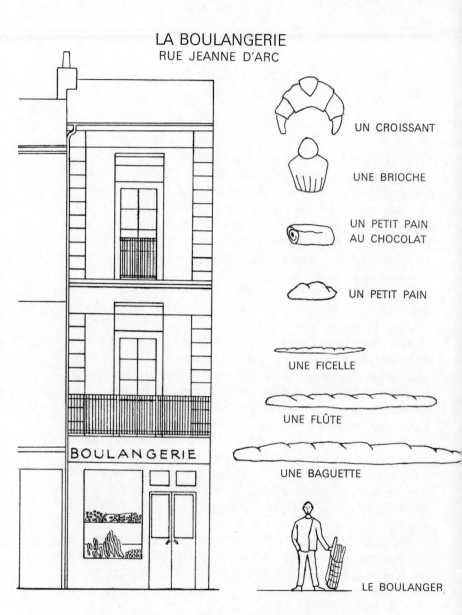

UN CROISSANT

UNE BRIOCHE

UN PETIT PAIN
AU CHOCOLAT

UN PETIT PAIN

UNE FICELLE

UNE FLÛTE

UNE BAGUETTE

LE BOULANGER

are too long to put in bags. A piece of tissue-paper may be wrapped round the bread where it is to be held, but if many loaves have to be carried to a **hôtel** or **café**, a special long wicker basket is used. Pre-sliced bread is not popular, although some bakers have special machines in their shop so that a loaf can be sliced at the moment of purchase. Bread is eaten with all meals, but it is so light and tasty that butter is rarely used. Sandwiches are made in a particular way. For example, **une flûte** is sufficient for four sandwiches. To begin with, a quarter of the loaf is cut off and sliced in half lengthways. The two halves are buttered and put together again when the filling has been added.

La Pâtisserie

La Pâtisserie is the cake shop. **Le pâtissier** makes his cakes on the premises, with the result that cakes vary slightly in size and price from shop to shop.

The picture shows some of the most popular **pâtisseries**. **Choux à la crème, religieuses,** and **éclairs** are made from **chou** pastry, which forms the light puffy casing of the cake. This casing has a special filling called **crème-pâtissière**, which is made with cornflour, eggs, milk, and sugar, with vanilla, coffee, or chocolate flavouring. Choux à la crème usually have a vanilla flavouring, whereas éclairs and religieuses have coffee or chocolate filling. Éclairs and religieuses also have a chocolate or coffee coating on top. **Chaussons** are made of puff pastry folded in half, and filled with stewed apple. A **baba au rhum** is sponge-cake soaked in rum syrup, possibly topped with a little fresh cream. **Moka chocolat** is light cake covered in coffee cream and sprinkled with small flakes of chocolate. Wafers are called **gaufrettes**, and one particular variety of these is **mille-feuille**, which is basically a large circular wafer folded over several times.

The many kinds of fruit tart include **tarte aux pommes, tarte aux abricots, tarte aux cerises,** and **tarte aux fraises.** The size of tarts varies a great deal, but the fruit is always carefully arranged in a uniform pattern.

Petits fours are miniature versions of pâtisseries, and **gâteau** is the usual word for large cakes which are cut into slices.

La pâtisserie may have a special room known as the **Salon de Thé** where customers can eat their cakes, having first chosen them from the shelves or from the trolley. Tea or coffee is served at the tables.

In many cases a pâtissier is also a **boulanger**, so that the sign over his shop reads **BOULANGERIE-PÂTISSERIE**. The sign **BOULANGERIE-CONFISERIE** indicates that the baker also sells sweets and chocolates. Le pâtissier sells ice-cream in addition to

LA PÂTISSERIE

cakes and may advertise this fact by having **PÂTISSIER-GLACIER** written above the shop window.

Cassata is an ice-cream which has fruit comfits in it, **napolitaine** is made of three separate flavours, **noisette** is an ice with hazel-nuts in it, and **moka** is coffee ice. Other ice-creams include **une glace à la vanille, une glace à la banane,** and **une glace aux fraises**.

In France, however, sweets and ice-creams are expensive, and children normally have them as a special treat.

Numéro 14

Les Maisons Particulières

French private houses are all different in design, and stand on their own. They are rarely semi-detached as in England. The house in the picture is only one example, of course, but it has several features which are typical.

UNE MAISON PARTICULIÈRE
RUE BARTHOLDI

The basement is the first item in the construction. It is made of worked stone and is the strongest part of the building. A basement is partially underground in most cases and serves several purposes. It provides an area for the garage, a space for the installation of the central-heating stove, storage space for fuel, a cellar for the wine, and perhaps a junk-room.

When the basement is finished wooden scaffolding, lashed together with rope, is erected in preparation for the main building. Although bricks are used for the walls, there is no sign of them in the picture. Many buildings in France have a smooth cement finish which conceals all the brickwork and drain-pipes which are often built into the wall to protect them against the extremely cold temperatures of winter. The cement finish also enables workmen to mould neat exterior frames round windows and doors.

Windows, which are sometimes double-glazed on the north side of the house, open inward and are adorned with shutters. Shutters can provide protection against very cold weather or too much sunshine, and even against passers-by looking in. By tradition, the design of shutters varies from region to region, as you can see from the map and the drawings, but it is not true to say that all shutters in one region are identical. Good shutters should be made from pine- or fir-trees in mountainous regions, and from oak elsewhere.

The last four drawings show other types of shutter which are frequently seen throughout France. **Un store Baumann** is made of slatted wood which unrolls from a hidden casing above the window. Its movement is guided by metal runners at the side of the window-frame. **Une persienne** (b) is composed of thin slats of wood mounted obliquely on a frame to let a little air and light into the room. The other sort of persienne (a) does not fold back against the wall. It is hinged in several places so that the panels fold neatly back against the window-frame. **Une jalousie** is made of a series of thin slats threaded on little chains, so that the angle of the slats may be varied as in a Venetian blind.

LA FRANCE
DES RÉGIONS GÉOGRAPHIQUES

LES VOLETS

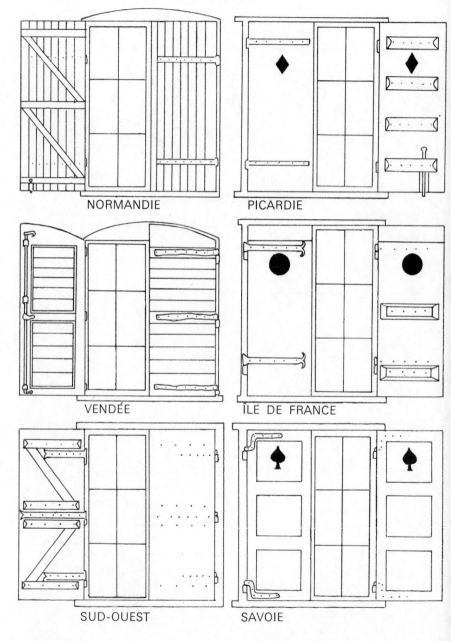

NORMANDIE PICARDIE

VENDÉE ÎLE DE FRANCE

SUD-OUEST SAVOIE

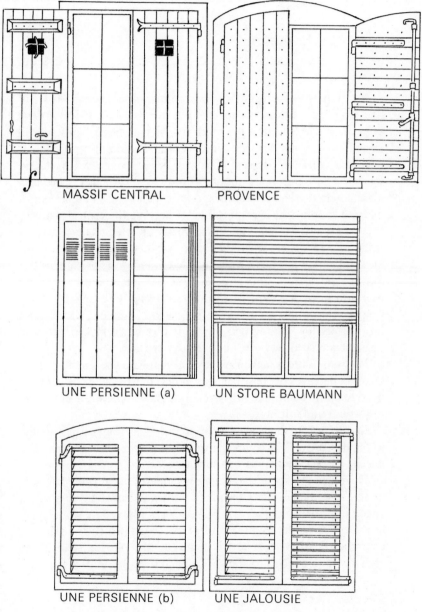

MASSIF CENTRAL PROVENCE

UNE PERSIENNE (a) UN STORE BAUMANN

UNE PERSIENNE (b) UNE JALOUSIE

Un Immeuble

Un appartement is a flat, and **un immeuble** is a block of flats. In French towns most people live in flats. Many blocks are the same as in England, but the more traditional ones are different in several ways. They have a **concierge** who lives on the ground floor near the entrance passage. The concierge is usually an elderly woman whose duties are similar to those of a caretaker. She has a man to help do the heavier work, or else the job may be shared by a married couple. She is responsible for keeping the central staircase and passageway clean, and often opens the electrically operated front door for callers when they ring. As she witnesses all the comings and goings she has a wide knowledge about the private lives of most of the tenants. On the other hand, tenants find the concierge useful to have on guard when they are away. The concierge may keep a pet because she lives on the ground floor, but flats are not ideal places for keeping pets, and this is one reason why cats and dogs are not seen very often in French towns.

The wall of the passageway may be lined with the tenants' letter-boxes. This saves the postman a great deal of trouble, as he does not need to climb stairs. He may even give the letters to the concierge to sort out and put in the boxes.

Some blocks of flats have common central heating, with the boiler in the basement. The concierge would be responsible for maintaining the correct temperature in such cases.

The block of flats in the picture is modern, but it is not the only kind. Some modern flats are much taller and may be step-shaped, becoming smaller as they get higher. Flats which date from stage-coach times have a central courtyard around which the flats are constructed. The courtyard is joined to the outside road by an archway high enough to allow a coach and horses to pass through.

UN IMMEUBLE
ANGLE COURS ST-JACQUES–CHEMIN DU COTEAU VERT

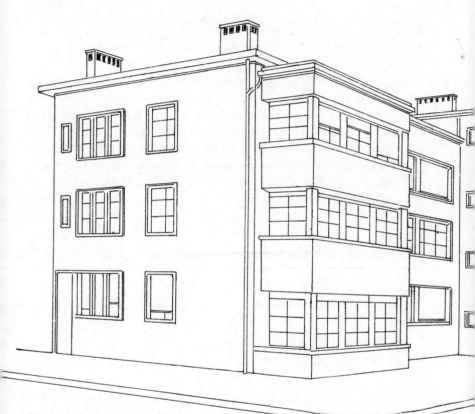

Numéro 16

Les Magasins d'Alimentation

Les Magasins d'Alimentation are shops which sell food and drink. We have already considered the bakers, and now we come to the other kinds of shopkeeper. In France a shopkeeper's name is usually of little importance on the legend above the shop-window. First place is given to his occupation, such as **Marchand de légumes** or **Épicier**, which would be written in large letters. In this way shoppers can see very clearly from a distance where the different sorts of shop are.

Numéro 16a

Le Poissonnier

Le Poissonnier is a fishmonger, and his shop is called **la poissonnerie**. The drawings show some of the fish that he sells. **La morue** (a) is cod, which is caught off Iceland and Newfoundland. Fresh cuts of cod are referred to as **cabillaud**. **Le saumon** (b) and **la truite** (c) are freshwater fish which are highly esteemed for their flavour. **Le merlan** (d), known in England as whiting, and **la sole** (e) are caught around the coast of France, although sole is found mainly in the Atlantic. **Une coquille St-Jacques** (f) is a scallop, **une huître** (g) is an oyster, and **une moule** (h) is a mussel. They are all shellfish which ought to be tightly closed when bought, as this is an indication of their freshness. They are found in the Atlantic and in the Channel near the French coast. Lobster, **le homard** (i), is another shellfish, but it is usually very expensive.

[48]

LE POISSONNIER

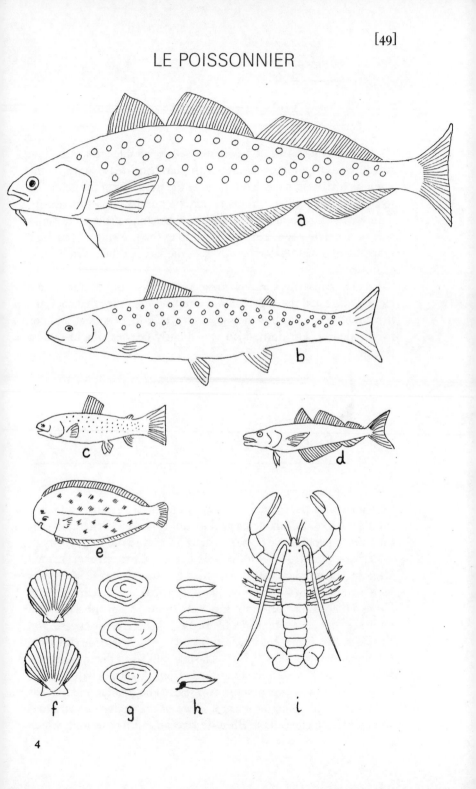

Numéro 16b

Le Marchand de Légumes

Le Marchand de Légumes sells vegetables and fruit. The word **Primeur** is often included with Marchand de Légumes on the name-board of the shop, to emphasize the freshness of the goods, or to indicate that certain products may be purchased out of season. The warm climate in France enables farmers to grow almost any sort of vegetable and fruit. For example, the growing of peaches, grapes, and tomatoes does not present the same problems in France as in Britain.

French housewives rarely make a purchase unless they have closely inspected the vegetables beforehand to ensure that they are firm and fresh. They buy their goods by the **kilo**, of course, and not by the pound. **Un demi-kilo** is a slightly heavier weight than a pound.

Numéro 16c

L'Épicier

L'Épicier is the grocer. His shop usually serves as the **crémerie** and the **laiterie** as well, where milk, cream, and dairy produce are sold. Milk delivery does not exist as in Britain, so that the French people have to make a daily journey to the shop to buy it.

Perhaps the best-known French cheese is **Camembert**, named after the village where it was created. The other twenty or so cheeses which come from Normandy, like **Demi-Sel** and **Fromage aux Fines Herbes**, are certainly less well known. Camembert is firm on the outside, but soft inside, Demi-Sel is a soft creamy cheese, and Fromage aux Fines Herbes is soft and blended with herbs. **Brie** is not made in Normandy, but its taste is similar to that of Camembert. It is usually sold in wedges cut from the large, flat, circular cheese. **Saint-Paulin** comes in two sizes. The smaller, red one has a wax-like rind which protects it. Two of the better known blue-veined French cheeses are **Bleu de Bresse** and **Roquefort**, which

LE MARCHAND DE LÉGUMES

is made from ewe's milk. **Gruyère** cheese originated in Switzerland, and is very popular in France now. It can be easily recognized by its large holes.

Vegetable oil is used extensively in cooking, as the French believe it is better for health than animal fat. This means that cooking oil is sold in great quantities, and is an item which is never missing from the shelf. Vinegar is also regarded as a necessity because it is mixed with oil to make salad dressings.

Tinned foods are as plentiful in France as in Britain. One unusual item is the packet of frozen snails, complete with frozen butter sauce. The shells may or may not be included in the packet. **Pâtes** are also seen more frequently in France than in Britain. They are really Italian in origin, made from flour and water. The names of pâtes are as numerous as their different shapes. **Ravioli, Spaghetti, Macaroni,** and **Vermicelle** are only a few of the various kinds.

Le supermarché is gradually establishing itself in France, taking over the functions of other shops besides **l'épicerie**.

Numéro 16d

Le Boucher et le Charcutier

Le Boucher is the butcher. In the drawings the cuts of meat which tend to be most popular in restaurants are shown. In the drawing of **le bœuf** (1), **entrecôtes** (a) are rib steaks, and the **contre-filet** (b) is known in Britain as the eye of the sirloin or upper fillet. It may be cut into steaks or served as a joint. The **romsteck** (c) provides fillet and rump steaks. Tender white meat comes from **le veau** (2). **Les côtes** (d) are chops which come from the rib. One of the most popular cuts of veal is **une escalope**, a thin boneless scallop or slice of lean meat. With regard to **le mouton** or **l'agneau** (3), **les côtes** (e) are chops and **les côtelettes** (f) are cutlets. **Le gigot** (g) is the leg, which is usually roasted. **Le porc** (4) also provides **côtes** (h), but it is better known for its ham, **jambon** (i), which comes from the legs.

French people occasionally eat horse and stag meat, which have a strong pleasant flavour. Horse meat is sold at a special shop known as **la boucherie chevaline**, easily distinguished by the horse symbol displayed outside. It should also be remembered that French butchers do not cut up the carcass of a beast in the same way as British butchers.

L'ÉPICIER

Le charcutier deals with prepared meats such as ham, tongue, sausage, and **pâté**. He also has a selection of prepared **hors-d'œuvre** and pies for sale. Sausages are of two kinds—**saucisse** and **saucisson**. Saucisse is usually made with minced pork and seasoning. It is usually known as fresh sausage, and has to be cooked. Saucisson is generally a much larger sausage which is already cooked. It is usually eaten cold, in slices. The drawing shows **cervelas** (j), which are saucisses, **saucissons de Morteau** (k), and a **saucisson à l'ail** (l). **Pâté** (m) is made from minced meat or minced liver, usually of pig or goose. It is a meat paste which may be soft enough to spread on bread, or firm enough to cut in slices. It may be cooked inside a crust like **pâté en croûte**, or made in a **terrine**, an earthenware dish, and protected by a thin coating of lard (such as **pâté**

terrine de foie gras). Pâté may also be presented as a sausage or plain without a crust.

Salade niçoise is only one of the prepared hors-d'œuvre which the charcutier sells. It is made from tomatoes, green peppers, French beans, anchovies, black olives, eggs, tuna fish, onion, olive oil, salt, and pepper. It is much easier for a housewife to buy this sort of hors-d'œuvre from the charcutier than to make it herself. Most charcutiers also sell savoury tarts such as **Pizza** and **Quiche lorraine**. Pizza is made of tomatoes, anchovies, black olives, and gruyère cheese, while Quiche lorraine is made from bacon and eggs.

Numéro 16e

Le Négociant en Vins

Le Négociant en Vins not only sells wine—the most important part of his job is the ordering of wine from the vineyards. This may entail making journeys to different parts of France to see the **viticulteurs** personally, so that he knows exactly what to expect from the yearly grape harvest. The good wine merchant has many friends among the vine-growers throughout France, and is an expert wine-taster.

The map shows four of the main wine-growing areas, and the bottles from left to right are from **Bordeaux, Bourgogne, Champagne**, and **Alsace**. The shape and colour of the bottles never vary. This is one means of recognizing wine in the shop. The glasses in the drawing, however, are only recommended. Champagne is really at its best when drunk from a tulip-shaped glass. Wines from Alsace should be drunk from tall, green-stemmed glasses. The glasses on the left are used for all other wines.

There are several wine-growing areas in the Bordeaux region. **Médoc** is situated north of Bordeaux, on the western side of the **Gironde**; **Graves** to the south of Bordeaux; **Sauternes** on the southern side of the **Garonne**; and **Entre-Deux-Mers** between the rivers Garonne and **Dordogne**. Red and white wines come from Bordeaux, the red in green bottles and the white wine in colourless bottles. White wine from this region is considered superior to the red wine, and the sweet white wine is said to be the best.

Red and white wines are also produced in Bourgogne. This region stretches about forty miles south along the **Route Nationale**

LE BOUCHER et
LE CHARCUTIER

74 from **Dijon**. This town is the capital of old Burgundy, although **Nuits St-Georges** and **Beaune** are the main centres of wine-growing. The northerly **Côte de Nuits** produces the better red wine, and the southerly **Côte de Beaune** the better white wine, of which the dry white is best. Burgundy is sold in green bottles.

The river **Marne** bisects the Champagne district, whose chief towns are **Reims, Épernay**, and **Châlons-sur-Marne**. Champagne is the northernmost part of France where grapes can be cultivated for wine. Champagne is a white wine which is always blended with an older white wine from the same area. A minute quantity of sugar is added to the wine before it is stored in bottles for a year. The presence of the sugar creates a gas which accounts for the sparkle or bubbles in the wine. Before being sent to the merchants the bottles are opened to release the sediment. At this stage a sugar syrup is added. The amount of sugary solution added makes Champagne either **doux**, which is very sweet, **demi-sec**, which is rather sweet, **sec**, rather dry, **extra-dry**, which is dry, or **brut**, which is very dry. The word dry (sec), of course, means the opposite of sweet. A corkscrew is not used to remove Champagne corks. The corks are held fast by wire which has to be untwisted for opening.

The wines of Alsace are white, and come in tall, elegant, green bottles. They are dry wines named after the grapes from which they are made. Some of the names are **Sylvaner, Riesling, Traminer, Gewürztraminer**, and **Muscat**. The best-known centres of this region west of the Rhine are **Colmar** and **Riquewihr**.

There are many other wine-growing areas in France. For example, the **Lorraine** wine-producing region is situated between the southern tips of the **Meuse** and **Moselle** rivers. Southern Burgundy is responsible for **Mâconnais** and **Beaujolais** wines. This region lies on the southern reaches of the **Saône** river. The wines of the **Côtes du Rhône**, of **Jura**, and of the **Midi** should not be forgotten. **Muscadet** is produced at the mouth of the river **Loire** in Brittany. This is a dry white wine. **Vouvray** comes from the **Touraine** region on the Loire, and the best **vin rosé** in France comes from **Anjou** in the Loire Valley.

Grapes are either white or black. White wine can be made from either kind of grape, but red wine is made only from black grapes. For white wine the skins of the grapes are removed immediately after pressing, because it is the skin which gives colour to wine. For red wine, however, the skins are left after pressing for several days, whereas the black skins are removed after several hours for vin rosé.

LE NÉGOCIANT EN VINS

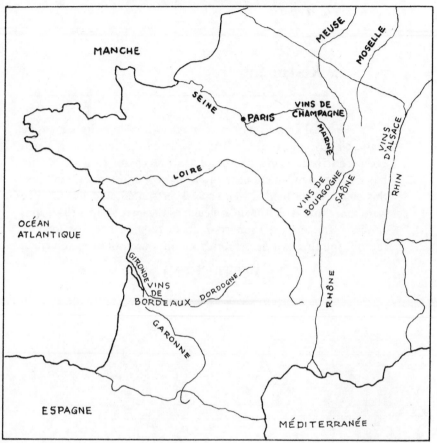

Le Restaurant

A meal in a French restaurant is usually more expensive than a comparable meal in a British restaurant, although it is worth every **centime**. Many restaurants in France are run as a family business. The members of the family work in the restaurant, and this ensures that food is well cooked, presented, and served. The waiters are just as skilful and efficient as the **garçon** in a **café**, and, similarly, they expect a reward of about 12 per cent of the total on the bill for their service. French families are not accustomed to

LE RESTAURANT
RUE VICTOR HUGO

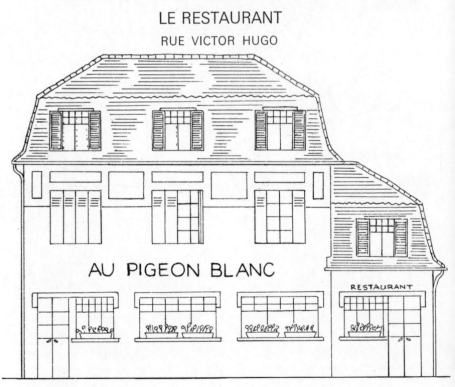

AU PIGEON BLANC

RESTAURANT

Sunday joints and Yorkshire puddings, but they tend to go to a restaurant for Sunday lunch. The **menu** and the prices are always displayed outside the restaurant. Customers can choose a set menu which offers a meal of several courses at a fixed price, sometimes known as the **plat du jour**. On the other hand, people who do not want a full meal, or who want something a little out of the ordinary, can make a selection **à la carte**, which is a list of separate dishes showing the price for each.

An example of an à la carte list at the **Pigeon Blanc** restaurant is shown below. The cooking terms are explained afterwards. Reference to **les magasins d'alimentation** will help you to understand the other words.

AU PIGEON BLANC
À LA CARTE

Couvert, vin, pain, et service: non compris

Hors-d'œuvre
Artichaut à la vinaigrette
Pâté en croûte
Radis au beurre
Sardines au beurre
Tomates à la vinaigrette
Saucisson à l'ail
Salade niçoise

Potages
Consommé au vermicelle
Potage à la bisque de homard
Soupe à l'oignon

Omelettes
Omelette parmentière
Omelette aux champignons
Omelette au jambon

Poissons
Merlan meunière
Sole Mornay
Moules à la marinière
Coquilles St-Jacques
Filet de cabillaud frit
Saumon froid
Truite au bleu, beurre fondu

Viandes

Contre-filet à la broche
Rôti de bœuf
Entrecôte grillée
Escalope de veau
Blanquette de veau
Médaillon de veau
Gigot d'agneau
Côtelette de mouton meunière
Côte de porc
Demi-poulet rôti

Spécialités

Escargots (la demi-douzaine)
Cuisses de grenouilles à la provençale

Légumes

Petits pois à la française
Petits pois au jambon
Haricots verts sautés
Haricots blancs
Tomates à la provençale
Riz
Pommes de terre frites
Pommes de terre à la lyonnaise
Pommes de terre sautées
Pommes de terre à l'anglaise

Salade

Fromage : le plateau

Dessert

Fruits de saison
Pâtisseries
Mousse au chocolat
Crème caramel

It is usual in France to have an **hors-d'œuvre** at lunch-time, and **potage** in the evening for dinner, but not both in the same meal. For the second course the choice is between **omelette** and **poisson**, but not usually both. This course is often omitted altogether, because the meal might be quite sufficient without it. The next course consists of meat, which is sometimes served separately from the vegetable course. The **spécialité** would, of course, replace the meat dish, although **escargots** sometimes have to be ordered a day in advance, especially in very small restaurants. The final course generally offers the choice of either **salade, fromage,** or **dessert.**

Cooking Terms

couvert:	the use of cutlery, place-mat, napkin, and glass sometimes has to be paid for.
hors-d'œuvre:	small snack served before the main meal.
à la vinaigrette:	with sauce made from a mixture of vinegar, oil, pepper, and salt.
potage:	the usual French word for soup.
consommé:	a light-coloured clear soup.
bisque:	a rich, thick, cream soup made from shellfish.
parmentière:	potato is included in the cooking.
meunière:	floured, seasoned, and fried in **beurre noir**.
beurre noir:	butter heated in the frying pan until it turns brown.
Mornay:	steamed in white wine with cheese sauce.
à la marinière:	boiled in water and wine with sliced onion.
frit(e)(s):	fried.
froid:	cold.
au bleu:	applied to fish cooked in fish stock, with wine added.
fondu:	melted.
à la broche:	roasted in front of a fire on a spit.
rôti:	roast or roasted.
grillée:	grilled.
blanquette:	stew with cream added.
médaillon:	round or oval-shaped pieces of meat.
poulet	chicken.
cuisse:	leg.
grenouille:	frog.
à la provençale:	fried in butter with garlic and parsley.
à la française:	boiled with lettuce-leaf and a clove of garlic.
sauté(e)(s):	partially boiled, then lightly fried in butter or oil.
à la lyonnaise:	fried with onions.
à l'anglaise:	steamed or boiled and served with butter.
salade:	when appearing by itself this word usually means **salade de laitue**.

La Poste

The post-office is referred to as **la poste** or the **P et T**. Some people still call it the **P.T.T.**, which used to stand for **Postes, Télégraphes, Téléphones**, although this is no longer the correct name.

The outside windows of the post-office are usually barred for security purposes. Two post-boxes, one marked **lettres** and the other marked **imprimés**, for printed matter, are set into the outside wall. These boxes are emptied more frequently than the other post-boxes in the town, and collection times are clearly shown. Sereinbourg post-office displays the following information:

HEURES DES LEVÉES
En Semaine

7.50	Régions: Paris, Lyon, Centre, Sud-Ouest
8.25	I. Distribution Ville
8.40	Poste Automobile Rurale
12.00	Toutes Destinations
14.00	Toutes Destinations
15.40	II. Distribution Ville
19.00	Régions: Paris, Reims, Nord-Ouest
19.20	Toutes Destinations

Dimanches et Jours Fériés
Néant

Stamp machines are fixed on the wall and may be one of several types. The instructions on the machines, however, always amount to the same thing:

1. Mettez une pièce de ... francs.
2. Attendez la chute des timbres.
3. Tirez le volet timbres-poste.

LA POSTE

RUE DES FLEURS

There is, of course, a place for the stamps to emerge, and a place for reimbursement (**remboursement**) in case the machine is empty or broken.

Inside the post-office the counters are usually divided into **guichets**. One guichet might be for buying and cashing money orders (**mandats**), another for making out telegrams (**télégrammes**), another for purchasing postage stamps (**timbres-poste**), another for the savings·bank (**caisse d'épargne**), and another for dispensing **jetons,** for the telephone. Callers have to purchase a jeton, which is a metal disc with a groove across one surface. It is the jeton which is put in the slot. If the post-office is closed callers have to find the nearest **café** or shop which sells·jetons. The thick volumes of telephone directories are firmly secured to their rack in the post-office, so that they cannot be removed. **Poste Restante** is a special facility for people who do not wish mail to be delivered by the postman. They can pay for their own letter-box in the post-office, and can go to collect their mail when they wish.

The drawings show **un taxiphone,** which is a public telephone. The taxiphone also has a post-box and a stamp machine, although these are out of sight in the picture. The postman, **le facteur,** usually carries his letters in a leather case slung across his shoulder. The detailed post-box on the left is blue. The newer type on the right is yellow, and warns against posting newspapers and printed matter. French post-boxes are very small and are usually fixed on walls, although some do stand on their own pedestal.

LA POSTE

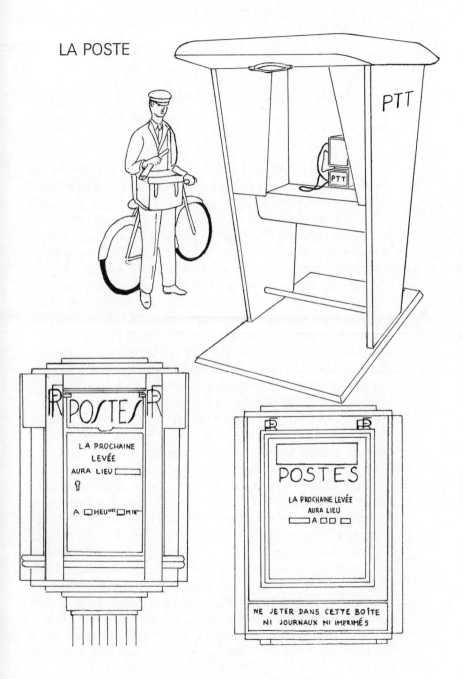

Numéro 19

Le Commissariat de Police et la Gendarmerie

Le Commissariat de Police is the Central Police Station for a town which has more than 10,000 inhabitants. The Chief Constable, **le commissaire de police**, is responsible to the **Préfet** of the **Département**, who is the Government representative of the region. **Le Poste de Police** is the part of the police station where daily routine work is done: lost property is reported, inquiries are made by the public, and policemen on duty telephone in.

A policeman is called **un agent de police**. He wears a navy-blue uniform with a black belt and cross-straps. The buttons of the tunic are embossed with an olive-branch across an oak-branch. This represents strength and peace, as it is the duty of a policeman to be **un gardien de la paix**. Policemen also wear a navy-blue **képi** which is a stiff, flat-topped cap. It has a very thin ribbon around the top edge. Policemen always carry a truncheon and a revolver, which, in the normal line of duty, is not loaded. On traffic duty the policeman exchanges his black belt, straps, and holster for white plastic ones. He also puts a wide white band round his képi, and uses white gauntlets. In this way he can be seen very easily by motorists.

La Gendarmerie is the police station in an area where there are no large towns. The one station serves several small villages and hamlets. Sereinbourg has a Gendarmerie because it is surrounded by many small scattered communities. The policemen who are based at a Gendarmerie are known as **gendarmes**. They are regarded as a military body on a national level. Although their uniform is similar to that of the agent de police, there are some differences. The tunic is black, the képi has a fairly broad white ribbon round the top edge, and the trousers are a lighter shade of navy blue. In the summer, however, gendarmes wear khaki. The **Garde Mobile** is also made up of gendarmes. As the name implies, this is the mobile section of the Gendarmerie, equipped with vans, cars, and motor-cycles.

[66]

LE COMMISSARIAT DE POLICE
RUE DE LA RÉPUBLIQUE

LA GENDARMERIE NATIONALE
RUE RÉCAMIER

The drawing of the policemen shows, from left to right, an agent de police, a member of the Garde Mobile, and a gendarme talking outside the Commissariat de Police.

LE COMMISSARIAT DE POLICE
ET
LA GENDARMERIE NATIONALE

POSTE DE POLICE

Numéro 20

L'Hôtel de Ville

L'Hôtel de Ville is the Town Hall, which may also be called **la Mairie**. L'Hôtel de Ville of Sereinbourg was built in the middle of the sixteenth century in the Renaissance style, and is therefore of historical and artistic interest as well as of political value. It is the seat of the Municipal Council, which is known as the **Conseil Municipal**.

Sereinbourg and the surrounding country communities make up a district which is called a **Commune**. All the people of the Commune over the age of twenty-one go to the voting booths every six years to elect the Conseil Municipal. The Conseil Municipal may have between eleven and thirty-seven members, depending on the size of the Commune. These councillors elect their leader from their own ranks, and he is called **le Maire** (the mayor). The councillors and the mayor are not paid for their work because they have ordinary jobs during the week. The mayor, however, is permitted an allowance if he needs it to meet expenses in the course of his mayoral duties. The mayor presides over council meetings when the Conseil Municipal has discussions and debates. The Conseil Municipal advises the mayor, and he puts the recommendations into force. He is responsible for everything in the Commune: the organization of municipal services such as parks and gardens; sanitation and roads; the administration of the property and land owned by the Commune; and the voting of the annual financial arrangements for the Commune. The mayor is responsible to the **Préfet** of the **Département**, whom he helps to ensure that the laws of the land are enforced. Special laws are sometimes required to meet particular local needs, and so the mayor can prepare by-laws which he puts before the Conseil Municipal for confirmation. The Préfet, however, has the right to disallow any by-law which the Government does not think suitable. It is clear, therefore, that the Conseil Municipal and the Maire do not have a completely free hand to administer the Commune exactly as they please. For example, although they can decide how to spend the money at their disposal for construction, repairs, and education, they are limited in the amount of money they are allowed each year. Their budget is decided by the **Conseil Général**.

Sereinbourg and its fourteen neighbouring Communes make up a region which is called a **Canton**. All the people over twenty-one in Sereinbourg and the whole Canton use their vote again every six years to elect a Conseil Général. The councillors of the Conseil Général meet twice a year to deal with money matters and decide the budget for each Commune. The Préfet of the Département has to approve the decisions of the Conseil Général, but once he has given his approval he has to ensure that its decisions are enforced. Like the Conseil Municipal, the Conseil Général cannot make decisions just as it wishes.

As the representative of the Government the Préfet is responsible for the police in the Département, and for advising local councils over which he can use his right of veto. He ensures that governmental decisions and laws are put into effect in his Département. He is appointed by the President of the French Republic, on the recommendation of the **Ministre de l'Intérieur** (Home Secretary). Each of the ninety Départements of France has a Préfet. He resides and works in the capital town (**la Préfecture**) of the Département.

Sereinbourg is in a Département which is divided into four **Arrondissements**. The Préfet has four assistants, who are called **Sous-Préfets**, and each one is in charge of an Arrondissement. In this Département an Arrondissement is composed of about seven Cantons, and each Canton has approximately fifteen Communes. Each Département in France is slightly different in size and composition, although they are all administered in the same way.

The inhabitants of Sereinbourg, the **Sereinbourgeois**, also take part in national elections. Every seven years all Sereinbourgeois over the age of twenty-one can vote in the Presidential election, and every five years they go to the polling booths to elect a **Député**, their Member of Parliament.

L'HÔTEL DE VILLE
PLACE DE LA NATION

HÔTEL DE VILLE

Numéro 21

La Station-Service

La Station-Service is a garage equipped to provide motor vehicles with petrol, oil, and water. It has facilities for greasing (**graissage**), washing down (**lavage**), and repairs. The petrol company which is concerned with the garage always has its name clearly marked on the buildings, although this is not shown in the drawing. A filling station which has only petrol-pumps and no other facilities is called **un poste d'essence**. A petrol-pump is **un distributeur d'essence**. Standard petrol is **ordinaire**, and premium petrol is **super-carburant**. The detailed face of a petrol-pump in the drawing shows all the information a customer needs—the quality of the petrol, the minimum quantity he can buy at any one time, and the price for each **litre**. As petrol is dispensed the price figures and the volume figures move simultaneously. Customers find it easier to state how many **francs** they wish to spend on petrol than to ask for a specific number of litres. This method is simpler for the petrol-pump attendant as well, because there are no odd bits of change to deal with.

LA STATION-SERVICE
RUE DE LA FORÊT

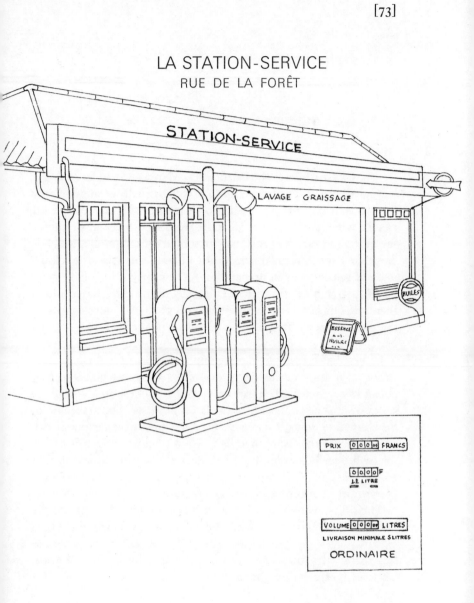

_____

Le Coiffeur

_____

Le Coiffeur is the hairdresser. Men who want an ordinary haircut ask for **une coupe ordinaire**, which usually means that only scissors and clippers are used. Some men prefer **une coupe au rasoir**, which needs the use of a razor. Razor-cutting really requires the hair to be wet, so it is usually preceded by a shampoo, which is known in French as **un shampooing**. The alternative way of cleaning and wetting hair in preparation for a razor-cut is to have hair-paraffin (**pétrole**) treatment. This does not involve water and is therefore quicker. Une coupe au rasoir is obviously more expensive than une coupe ordinaire, but it is considered better for styling the hair.

Ladies' hairdressing is more complicated because of the greater variety of styles. The drawing shows nine styles in which hair can be cut and set. A set is called **une mise en plis**. These are the kinds of styles which persist in spite of the latest fashions. The first four are for **cheveux courts**. Customers need not go into long explanations about the way they want their hair to look. One or two words suffice for each one. For example, the following descriptions are all that are necessary: A—**avec une frange**; B—**tirés en arrière**; C—**raides et géométriques**; D—**frisés**.

The other five styles are for **cheveux longs**. Once again, the hairdresser would understand short, precise explanations. These explanations would be adequate: E—**avec une frange, et une raie au milieu**; F—**bouclés**; G—**chignon très haut**; H—**chignon bouclé**; I—**queue de cheval**.

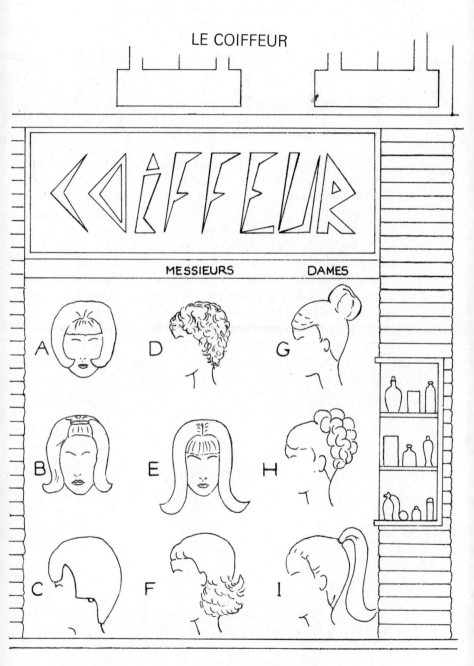

Le Cinéma et le Théâtre

Sereinbourg has two cinemas—the **Studio-Serein** on the **Boulevard Gambetta** and the **Palace** in **Place de la Nation**. Cinema names are numerous, but **Rex, Cinéac, Lux, Royal, Gaumont, Palais, Olympic,** and **Pax** are a few of the more common ones. Some names like **Studio, Ciné,** and **Royal** are often linked to another word to make up the title. Since 1895, when moving pictures were first shown to public audiences, cinema techniques have naturally improved. A cinema can now advertise **un film en couleurs,** and **écran large** or **écran géant.** Smoking is not permitted in the auditorium, and one is often expected to give a small tip to the usherette. Some films are forbidden to children of less than thirteen years, some to those less than sixteen years, and some to those less than eighteen years. The price of seats and the times of performances at the **Studio-Serein** are shown opposite:

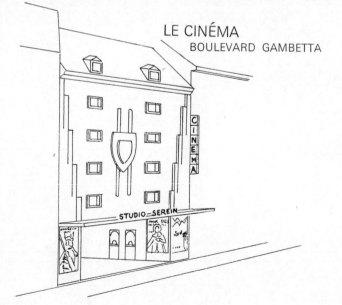

LE CINÉMA
BOULEVARD GAMBETTA

Places	*Prix*	*Séances*
Orchestre	fr.	En Semaine:
		14h20, 16h50,
Balcon	fr.	19h20, 22h.

Tarif Réduit	Samedi, Dimanche, Fêtes:
En Semaine: Étudiants	Permanent à partir de
Jeudi: Enfants	13h40 jusqu'à 24h.

The **orchestre** is downstairs, and the **balcon** is upstairs. Students and schoolchildren can sometimes get in at a reduced rate. **Séances** are the performances. Small cinemas are usually emptied after each showing of the film, but the word **permanent** means that the film is shown continuously.

Le Théâtre Municipal was built in the late eighteenth century in the French classical style. In addition to serious plays, musical comedies (**opérettes**) are produced. The theatre is also used for lectures and musical concerts, and, owing to its large seating capacity, it is ideal for performances given by visiting singers, either in the **chansonnier** tradition or of the popular variety.

Tipping the usherette is more usual here than in the cinema, and the smoking ban is as strict. Programme and ice-cream sellers call out **"Demandez un programme"** and **"Demandez une glace"** before the play begins and during the **entr'acte**.

The seating arrangements in the theatre are more complex than in the cinema. The stalls are **les fauteuils d'orchestre**; the ground-floor boxes are **les baignoires** or **les loges**; the circle is **le balcon**. Higher up is the gallery, called **l'amphithéâtre** or **la galerie**; highest of all is **le paradis**, which we call the gods; and **la loge d'avant-scène** is the stage box on the same level as the circle.

LE THÉÂTRE
RUE DU THÉÂTRE

La Maison de la Presse

La Maison de la Presse is the newsagent's shop, **la Librairie** is the book-shop, and **la Papeterie** is the stationery shop. Many newsagents deal in books and stationery in addition to newspapers.

Thirteen daily newspapers are printed in Paris for sale throughout France. A daily paper is **un quotidien**. Six of the Parisian ones appear in the drawing. **L'Aurore** is the newspaper which appeals mainly to middle-class tradesmen. **Combat** is an intellectual paper for Socialists. **Le Figaro** is politically inclined to the right, traditional and quietly respectable. **France-Soir** is the most popular evening paper in France and has a circulation of over a million. It is rather sensational. **L'Humanité** is a very important Communist daily. **Le Monde** is a serious, intellectual, unbiased newspaper which has no pictures and is always dated for the day after it is printed and sold. A daily sports paper is also printed in Paris. This is called **L'Équipe**, in which every kind of sport is represented.

Newspapers are also printed in other parts of France. There are 110 provincial papers, of which **Ouest-France, Le Progrès de Lyon, le Dauphiné Libéré, La Voix du Nord,** and **La Dépêche de Toulouse** are the best known. A very popular weekly paper is shown in the drawing. This is **Le Canard Enchaîné**, which describes itself as **un journal satirique**, making fun of politicians and their policies.

A weekly publication is called **un hebdomadaire**. There are literally thousands of different magazines, but only two are shown here. **Paris-Match** is one of the most popular illustrated weeklies of general interest, and **Elle** is one of the most successful women's magazines.

LA MAISON DE LA PRESSE

LIBRAIRIE PAPETERIE

LE FIGARO

France-Soir

L'AURORE

Le Monde

Le Canard
enchaîné

l'Humanité

ELLE

PARIS
MATCH

L'EQUIPE

✝ COMBAT

L'Hôtel

It is safest for travellers to stay at hotels which are registered with the **Syndicat d'Initiative** because the Syndicat publishes details of such hotels. With a hotel list in front of him the traveller can see exactly what to expect for the price. There are five categories of hotel. The most expensive are luxury and four-star hotels. Three-, two-, and one-star hotels are further subdivided into A, B, and C classes. The very best rooms have their own bathroom or shower and w.c. However, even the meanest room usually has its own washbasin curtained off. The price of a double room is less than twice the price of a single room, and these prices are generally much cheaper than in Britain. All rooms should have the price displayed on the back of the door or somewhere where it can easily be seen. The cost of breakfast, the service charge, and the local taxes should also be shown. Visitors may have full **pension**, which includes bed, breakfast, lunch, and dinner, or **demi-pension**, which is bed, breakfast, and one other meal. Hotels which have every comfort and central heating are advertised **Tout Confort, Chauffage Central**. Most hotels have their own bar, and the larger ones have their own **café** and **restaurant** as well, like the **Hôtel Métropole** in Sereinbourg.

L'HÔTEL
ANGLE RUE ROBESPIERRE–RUE DE LA FORÊT

L'Église, la Place du Marché, et les Magasins

L'Église Saint-Jacques, an example of Romanesque architecture, was built in 1150. All the different times of **Messe** at the church are written on a sign shaped like a cross which is placed by the side of each road leading into Sereinbourg. On Sundays when all the families converge on the church the **Place du Marché** serves as a very convenient car-park.

Market days are Tuesdays and Fridays. Farmers and tradespeople from the surrounding district of Sereinbourg bring their produce and stock to the Place du Marché to sell at prices which compete with those of the local shops. The stalls are set up in the middle of the square, allowing enough space for traffic to pass round the edges. Tuesdays and Fridays are therefore very busy times, with people bustling about, money changing hands, and voices raised.

During the rest of the week the Sereinbourg shopkeepers do not have any competition. In any case, it is unlikely that the **Grand Magasin** is affected at all by the presence of the market. As in Britain, the department store stocks a very wide range of goods, and is probably a member of a large company. Also in great demand are shops like **Monoprix**, **Uniprix**, and **Prisunic**, which, as their names imply, sell goods cheaply.

Un magasin or **une maison d'ameublement** is a furniture shop, and **un magasin d'appareils électroménagers** deals in electrical goods, and even records. **La Quincaillerie** is the hardware shop, and **la Droguerie** sells household cleaning equipment. **La Pharmacie**, the chemist's, is clearly indicated by a large white-and-green cross within a circle. Articles bought on a doctor's prescription should have a gummed price label attached. Customers have to remove the label, which is called **une vignette**, and keep it until they make their claim for reimbursement from the **Sécurité Sociale**. Cosmetics and perfumes are sold at **la Parfumerie**, not at the chemist's. Leather goods are sold at **la Maroquinerie**, and are generally more plentiful than in Britain. **Cuir** is the word for leather, **peau de chèvre** is goatskin, and **daim** is suède.

There are, of course, many other shops in Sereinbourg, some of which have been mentioned earlier in this book. Indeed, the best way of feeling the atmosphere in the town is to wander around the shops on a Tuesday or a Friday and end up at la Place du Marché. The atmosphere does not change very much from season to season, nor from year to year, although there is a rumour that a new town is planned for near by very soon.

A new town is called **une ville bis**, and these are being designed and built at many places throughout France. Large and small towns alike are having these new and necessary additions. Une ville bis provides more housing and employment for the rising population, and new industrial sites for the strengthening of the economy.

VUE DE L'ÉGLISE
ET DE LA PLACE DU MARCHÉ

Classroom Activities

Introduction
Le Plan de la Ville

1. Draw your own plan of an imaginary town. Think carefully about how and where your town was established, so that you can build it up in the correct way. One or two rough plans may have to be drawn up before you are finally satisfied.
2. Find out whom the streets of Sereinbourg are named after. For example, **Boulevard Gambetta** is named after a famous French politician, and **Cours St-Jacques** is named after a saint.
3. Choose suitable names for the main streets of the town which you have planned.

Numéro 1
La Gare

1. Draw a plan of a French railway station with a key, and arrange the amenities, facilities, and offices in the way which you think would be most efficient for the day-to-day running of the station.
2. Make brief notes of the facts in the text, and add notes which your teacher has given you. There is no need to write sentences, but make your notes very clear.
3. Mark in **La Gare** on your town plan.

Numéro 2
La Gare d'Autobus et la Gare Routière

1. What is the difference between these two sorts of bus station?
2. Write notes on the differences between buses in France and buses in Britain.
3. Draw a French bus and decide upon a colour scheme for the exterior.
4. Mark in **La Gare d'Autobus** and **La Gare Routière** on your town plan.

Numéro 3
Le Syndicat d'Initiative

1. Explain the purpose of a **Syndicat d'Initiative**.
2. Make a drawing of a **Syndicat d'Initiative**.
3. Select a spot for the S.I. on your town plan.

[84]

Numéros 4, 5, 6, et 7

Les Écoles

1. Make notes about the people who work in French schools and add notes which your teacher has given you.
2. Write down the French names for the six classes in a **lycée**.
3. Draw a picture of a teaching block at a **lycée**.
4. Compare your timetable for Tuesday with the equivalent time-table for a French school.
5. Mark the four different kinds of school on the town plan.

Numéro 8

Le Parc

1. Select a suitable area in the town for a park.
2. Draw a plan of a park, arranging the details to your liking, and make a key for it.

Numéro 9

Le Café

1. Draw a picture of a French **café** and its terrace. Then add the glass partition as for winter-time. Choose a name for the **café**.
2. Imagine that you are a waiter who is serving at four tables. The first table has two people, the second table has three people, the third table has five people, and the fourth table has six people. Decide which drink each customer has ordered and make up an imaginary bill for each table. Remember to add the service charge.
3. Select nine places in the town where you would like to put a **café**.

Numéro 10

La Rue

1. Draw a street in cross-section, making the pavement wide so that you have enough space to put in all the items. Put a letter by each item you draw and put the key underneath. You should include **le trottoir** and **la bouche d'égout**, in addition to the names given in the text.
2. If your picture does not explain everything you should write one or two sentences about the characteristics of a French street to make it clear what you mean.

Numéro 11
La Signalisation Routière

1. Select eight of the French road signs and draw them. Make sure that you use the correct colours.
2. Draw three French road signs which are not included in this chapter, one from each group.

Numéro 12
La Boulangerie

1. Make drawings of the baker's wares.
2. Explain how a **croissant** is made.
3. How can you tell if a French loaf is fresh?
4. What is **le goûter**?
5. Select five possible sites for bakeries in the town.

Numéro 13
La Pâtisserie

1. Make drawings of the cakes.
2. Explain what **chou** pastry and **crème-pâtissière** are.
3. Explain the meaning of BOULANGERIE-PÂTISSERIE, PÂTISSERIE-CONFISERIE, PÂTISSIER-GLACIER.
4. Select five possible sites for cake-shops on the plan of the town.

Numéro 14
Les Maisons Particulières

1. Make a simple drawing of a private house and label the following items:

   (a) **le faîtage**   (g) **le porche**
   (b) **la cheminée**   (h) **la porte**
   (c) **le toit**   (i) **le perron**
   (d) **le mur**   (j) **le garage**
   (e) **la fenêtre**   (k) **le soubassement**
   (f) **le volet**

2. Draw: (a) **un volet**; (b) **un store**; (c) **une persienne**; (d) **une jalousie**.
3. By consulting a suitable atlas discover which of the regional shutters should be made of oak and which should be made of pine or fir.
4. Mark out suitable areas in the town for private houses.
5. Make a list of the uses of a basement in a French house.

Numéro 15

Un Immeuble

1. Make a drawing of a block of flats.
2. Write down all you can about a **concierge**.
3. Mark in as many blocks of flats as you think necessary on the town plan.

Numéro 16*a*

Le Poissonnier

1. Make drawings of the following fish to show the differences between them: **une morue, un saumon, une truite, un merlan, une sole.**
2. Mark three fish-shops on the town plan.

Numéro 16*b*

Le Marchand de Légumes

1. Find out the exact weight of **un kilo.**
2. Draw the following fruits and vegetables, beginning with the ones you know best: **de l'ail, un artichaut, une banane, une carotte, une cerise, un champignon, un chou, un chou-fleur, des haricots blancs, un haricot vert, un melon, un oignon, une orange, des petits pois, une poire, un poivron vert, une pomme, une pomme de terre, un radis, une tomate.**
3. Mark three greengrocery shops on the town plan.

Numéro 16*c*

L'Épicier

1. Try to find any of the articles in the drawing by looking through a French magazine. Make a classroom display of articles found in a grocer's shop, using suitable advertisements, drawings, or empty packets.
2. Select ten items of groceries to draw and label.
3. Choose three places for grocery shops and two sites for supermarkets on the plan of the town.

Numéro 16*d*

Le Boucher et le Charcutier

1. Briefly explain the differences between **un boucher** and **un charcutier**.
2. Explain the following words: **une côte, une côtelette, une entrecôte, un contre-filet, un gigot, du jambon, une escalope**.
3. Draw and explain the different kinds of sausages and meat pastes.
4. Select and mark three suitable places for butchers' shops in the town.

Numéro 16*e*

Le Négociant en Vins

1. Draw an outline map of France and mark in the four wine-producing areas mentioned in the text.
2. Make brief notes about one of the wine-producing areas shown on your map.
3. Explain in your own words how wine is coloured.
4. There are three wine merchants in Sereinbourg. Indicate where they have their shops on your town plan.

Numéro 17

Le Restaurant

1. Read the rules for compiling a **menu** very thoroughly and make up a set **menu** in French for a midday meal. Select only one dish for each part of the meal.
2. Explain the **menu** which you have just made up for the benefit of an English person who does not understand French.
3. Give a price for the **menu** and add the service charge.
4. If four people together at one table have all ordered your **menu** work out the overall price you should charge them.
5. Make up a different set **menu** for an evening meal. Select two dishes for each part of the meal so that the customers can have a choice.
6. Explain your **menu** to an English tourist.
7. Give a price for the **menu** and add the service charge.
8. If three people in a party all order your **menu**, what will the overall price be?
9. Choose seven places in the town to mark as restaurants.

Numéro 18

La Poste

1. What items would you expect to see on the outside wall of a post-office?
2. Draw a French post-box and show the wording on it.
3. Make some notes about the French post-office concerning aspects which are not the same as in Britain.
4. Mark the post-office on the town plan.

Numéro 19

Le Commissariat de Police et la Gendarmerie

1. How do the authorities decide where a **Commissariat de Police** is necessary?
2. With the help of coloured drawings explain the differences in appearance between **un agent de police** and **un gendarme**.
3. Show the positions of the **Commissariat de Police** and the **Gendarmerie** on your plan of the town.

Numéro 20

L'Hôtel de Ville

1. Draw a diagram to show how a **Département** is divided into **Arrondissements, Cantons,** and **Communes**.
2. Make notes to show that you have understood how the **Conseil Municipal** and **le Maire** govern a **Commune**.
3. Select a site for the Town Hall on your plan.

Numéro 21

La Station-Service

1. What is the difference between **une station-service** and **un poste d'essence**?
2. If your teacher tells you the price of petrol in France estimate how many **litres** you can buy for twenty **francs**.
3. Make a list of the different French firms which make cars and lorries.
4. Draw the outline of a car and label the following parts: **la roue, la portière, le pare-brise, le phare, le coffre, le capot, le pneu**.
5. Try to find some pictures of French cars which you can draw. Give the name for each one.
6. Mark seven places on the town plan for petrol stations.

Numéro 22
Le Coiffeur

1. In men's hairdressing what is the difference between **une coupe ordinaire** and **une coupe au rasoir**?
2. Draw and label four ladies' styles for either short or long hair.
3. Select three places on the town plan for hairdressers' shops.

Numéro 23
Le Cinéma et le Théâtre

1. Find out the names of some French film stars.
2. With the help of a diagram explain the seating arrangements of the theatre in Sereinbourg.
3. Find sites in the town for two cinemas and one theatre.

Numéro 24
La Maison de la Presse

1. Explain what type of person would reach each of the newspapers.
2. If you can find a copy of **L'Équipe** make a list in French of all the sports it covers.
3. What is **une librairie** and **une papeterie**?
4. Mark five **Maisons de la Presse** on your plan of the town.

Numéro 25
L'Hôtel

1. Make a list of all the different categories and classes of hotel.
2. Explain the meaning of **pension** and **demi-pension**.
3. Mark five hotels on your town plan.

Numéro 26
L'Église, la Place du Marché, et les Magasins

1. Draw the scene of the market place on market day.
2. Write down the names of some **Grands Magasins** in France.
3. Make a classroom display showing goods which can be bought in the following shops: **un magasin d'appareils électro-ménagers, un magasin d'ameublement, la maroquinerie, la quincaillerie,** and **la droguerie.** Use can be made of advertisements from French magazines.
4. Find some advertisements concerning **la Parfumerie** and make a list of cosmetics in French.
5. Find a suitable situation for the church in the town, and try to find spaces for some shops. Each kind of shop you add to the plan will need its own number, with a special key to explain it.

Notes and Suggestions for the Teacher

It is suggested that classroom activities follow the same basic pattern in each section of the book. In the first instance the text is read aloud round the class and the picture is considered. Discussion may arise, and the teacher has the opportunity of adding his knowledge to the facts contained in the text. It is recommended that any suitable visual aid should be used at the appropriate time to make the French town become more real in the eyes of the children. The children then draw their picture, make notes or write sentences, and mark the items on the town plan. Children should be encouraged from the outset to take great care with their pictures and writing. The guided use of crayons for the drawings may lend added interest to the work.

Introduction

Le Plan de la Ville

A large plan of an imaginary town drawn by the teacher could be pinned to the wall as a fairly permanent fixture. Each item in the town could be marked on as it is dealt with. Such a plan would act as a guide to the children when they consider where to mark the different buildings on their own plan, and it would be useful to children who have been absent, in helping them to see what they have missed. Without this different, larger plan children might be tempted to copy the one in the book.

In Question 2 of the activities section the teacher may prefer to select only ten of the street names for children to identify. It would be an arduous and pointless task for a child to find out about all the names.

It might prove useful to explain briefly the differences between **boulevard, avenue, rue, chemin, cours,** and **place**.

Numéro 1

La Gare

Posters or pictures of a French train or any aspect of a railway station could be put on the wall to give children a feeling of the atmosphere of life at a French station. Children might be able to make drawings from suitable pictures.

Numéro 2

La Gare d'Autobus et la Gare Routière

You may be able to supply for the children a list of the firms which manufacture buses and coaches.

Some French posters show a French bus as an incidental detail of the picture. This could be displayed on the classroom wall.

Any advertisements for French coaches which you find in magazines might prove useful to show that buses are not all the same.

Double-decker buses were put into service in Paris in 1967. Developed for the **R.A.T.P. (Régie autonome des Transports parisiens)**, these buses can carry 94 passengers. The Red Arrow bus service was introduced in London in 1966 as an experiment. The single-deck buses used in this service have more room for standing than for sitting. There is no conductor, and passengers pay a fixed fare into an automatic coin machine. There is room for 73 passengers.

Numéro 3

Le Syndicat d'Initiative

If you have any souvenir pamphlets and maps from your travels in France you could show them to the children. If you have a particular memory or photograph of a special **Syndicat d'Initiative** you could draw this on the blackboard for the children to copy.

Numéros 4, 5, 6, 7

Les Écoles

You may be in a position to supply much information relevant to this subject. Special school terms and school slang might be of interest to the children.

Numéro 8

Le Parc

A plan of Paris could be displayed and the parks and woods pointed out to the children.

Bartholdi could provide scope for some personal research on the part of the children.

Numéro 9
Le Café

In Question 2 of the activities section children will need to know the approximate price of refreshments. This could easily be dealt with by making a list on the blackboard of the different categories of drink, such as **café, infusion, boisson gazeuse**, with the price in francs for each category. Accurate estimates of current prices would, of course, be more realistic.

Numéro 10
La Rue

Other aspects of a French street which you think warrant a mention could be explained when the text has been read round the class. Characteristics of Parisian streets or of a particular region would be of interest.

Numéro 11
La Signalisation Routière

Question 2 depends entirely on the teacher for the necessary information.

Numéro 12
La Boulangerie

Additional information concerning other wares may be considered desirable.

Numéro 13
La Pâtisserie

Additional information concerning other wares may be considered desirable.

Numéro 14
Les Maisons Particulières

As many pictures of French private houses as possible will help in giving a better idea of French architecture, thereby enabling the children to draw more realistic pictures for Question 1.

Numéro 15
Un Immeuble

Since blocks of flats can vary so much in design, as many different pictures as possible would help children to receive a better idea of what is needed in Question 1.

Numéro 16
Les Magasins d'Alimentation

The five **magasins d'alimentation** are primarily intended as a preparation for the restaurant. If you wish to modify the **menu**, or add to it when dealing with **Numéro 17: Le Restaurant**, preparation for it should take place now. For example, other names for fish, vegetables, and meat should be added in the suitable sections if you wish to include them in the **menu**.

Numéro 16a
Le Poissonnier

Numéro 16b
Le Marchand de Légumes

Children may not be clear about **haricots blancs** and **haricots verts** when they are drawing vegetables. **Haricots verts**, of which the pod and the bean are both eaten, are longer and thinner than the pod of **haricots blancs**, of which only the bean itself is edible.

Numéro 16c
L'Épicier

Normandy is mentioned in connection with cheese. The teacher may feel that more could be said about cheese, especially if there is suitable illustrated information about it ready to hand. The teacher should be prepared to provide the necessary materials for the first activity.

Numéro 16d
Le Boucher et le Charcutier

Numéro 16e
Le Négociant en Vins

A suitable selection of wine-bottles for children to have a look at might prove interesting.

Numéro 17
Le Restaurant

If you wish to modify the **menu** in this section you may find it necessary to add to the list of cooking terms. Children will depend upon their teacher for prices in Questions 3 and 7. This only involves giving a realistic figure for a set **menu**.

Numéro 18

La Poste

Prices are avoided in the text. Greater realism would be achieved if the teacher could supply current prices of the **jeton** and stamps.

Numéro 19

Le Commissariat de Police et la Gendarmerie

Pictures of policemen, especially if police vehicles are included, might add interest.

Numéro 20

L'Hôtel de Ville

The drawing shows **un hôtel de ville** built in the Renaissance style. This has been done for 'atmosphere', and also in case the teacher wishes to deal with architecture at greater length. (Examples of Romanesque and Classical architecture appear later on.) The features of Renaissance architecture shown in the drawing include the first-floor windows, the columns or shafts, the quarry-stone arranged in a certain way, the caryatids (statues of women used as supports like columns), and the ornamental relief work. The way the French Parliamentary system works has been avoided here, in order to cause as little confusion as possible. Some classes, however, may be ready to understand the **Exécutif** and the **Législatif**. Mention might also be made of civil marriages. Some guidance will probably be necessary in drawing the diagram for Question 1.

Numéro 21

La Station-Service

The price of a **litre** of petrol is required in Question 2. The teacher's help will also be required in Question 3. Some children may be able to produce model cars for drawing or advertisements of French cars. Car registration numbers might be of interest.

Numéro 22

Le Coiffeur

Additional hair styles for women may be introduced, with the appropriate descriptions in French.

Numéro 23

Le Cinéma et le Théâtre

The diagram of seating arrangements in the theatre may need the teacher's guidance. The drawing of the theatre shows a building in the French Classical style. Largely inspired by Greek and Roman architecture, its features include a generally grand, harmonious, and austere appearance, columns supporting the architrave, very tall windows on the first floor, and **œil-de-bœuf** windows higher up.

Numéro 24

La Maison de la Presse

The seven Parisian papers not in the drawing are **La Croix, Les Échos, Journal Officiel de la République Française, Libération, Paris-Journal, Paris-Presse l'Intransigeant,** and **Le Parisien Libéré**. It should be possible to acquire several different French newspapers which could be shown to the children. **L'Équipe** would be necessary for Question 2.

Numéro 25

L'Hôtel

Mention could be made of the registration card which foreigners normally have to fill in at the hotel.

Numéro 26

L'Église, la Place du Marché, et les Magasins

The church is an example of Romanesque architecture. So that the walls are not weakened, the larger windows are divided into two by a small column, and the smaller windows are narrower on the outside than on the inside. The Gothic style of architecture is not represented in the town.

A poster showing the bustle of market day would help the children with their drawing in Question 1. It is not likely that the children will be able to find out for themselves the particular names of the department stores in France. Once again, the teacher will have to provide the children with suitable material for display.